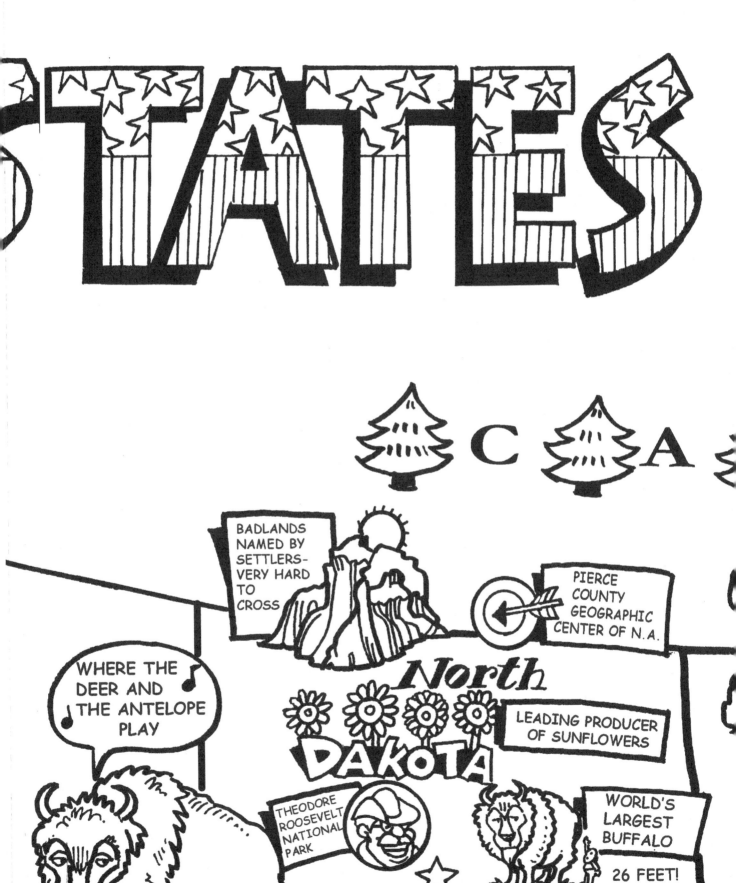

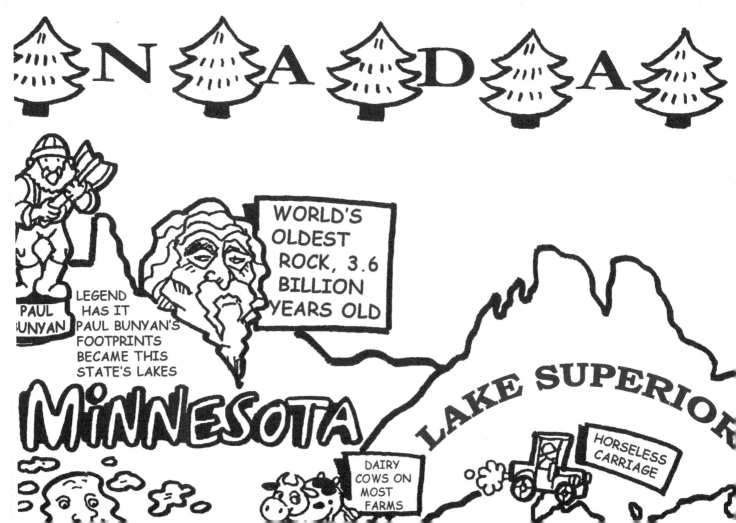

PAUL BUNYAN

LEGEND HAS IT PAUL BUNYAN'S FOOTPRINTS BECAME THIS STATE'S LAKES

WORLD'S OLDEST ROCK, 3.6 BILLION YEARS OLD

MINNESOTA

LAKE SUPERIOR

DAIRY COWS ON MOST FARMS

HORSELESS CARRIAGE

ERICA

CANADIAN GEESE

HONK

H URON
O NTARIO
M ICHIGAN
E RIE
S UPERIOR

GREAT LAKES

ENGLAND COVERED BRIDGES

MARBLE QUARRIES

AUGUSTA

LAKE CHAMPLAIN LEGENDARY MONSTER "CHAMP"

MONTPELIER

10 MILLION TOURISTS A YEAR!

INVENTED EAR MUFFS

CAPE COD WHALE WATCHING

New Hamp-shire

1 GAL.

4 TREES = 1 GAL. SYRUP

MASS. DR. SEUSS

MASS. 1ST LIGHT-HOUSE 1718

NEW YORK

VERMONT

CONCORD

NAT. ROTTEN SNEAKER CHAMPIONSHIP

ALBANY

OME OF K. BAUM

BOSTON

MASSACHUSETTS

CRANBERRY BOGS

R.I. 1ST AUTO PARADE

ST R.R. 11 MILES LONG

PLYMOUTH ROCK 1620.

1ST GOLF COURSE

1st ZOO PA

EMPIRE STATE BUILDING STRUCK BY LIGHTNING MORE THAN ANY OTHER BUILDING!

HARTFORD

R.I.

PROVIDENCE

48 MILES LONG, 37 MILES WIDE

R.I. 1ST ROLLER SKATING RINK

T!

CONNECTICUT

STATUE OF LIBERTY

HERSHEY HOME OF CANDY BAR

CLAM CHOWDER

1st HOT DOG WAS A DACHSUND DOG ON CONEY ISLAND

WILD COYOTES NARRAGANSETT BAY.

NEW JERSEY

THE TURKEY ALMOST BECAME OUR NATIONAL SYMBOL!

BENJAMIN FRANKLIN

TRENTON

THOMAS EDISON MENLO PARK

354 STEPS TO CROWN

EDGAR A. POE WROTE THE RAVEN

GARDEN STATE

N. JERSEY MISS AMERICA BEAUTY PAGEANT, ATLANTIC CITY

1ST DINOSAUR SKELETON FOUND IN 1858 NEW JERSEY

MONOPOLY GAME BOARD HAS THE STREET NAMES FROM ATLANTIC CITY!

SALT WATER TAFFY

SUBMARINES

CONNECTICUT

DOVER

STATE DELAWARE 1ST

land

WILD PONIES OF ASSATEAGUE ISLAND

APOLIS

THE STAR SPANGLED BANNER WAS FROM A POEM "DEFENCE OF FORT McHENRY"

DEL. BLUE HEN CHICKEN

PIRATE REENACTMENT IN HAMPTS

HORSESHOE

CAPE HATTERAS, N. CAROLINA

GRAVEYARD OF THE ATLANTIC THOUSANDS OF SUNKEN SHIPS

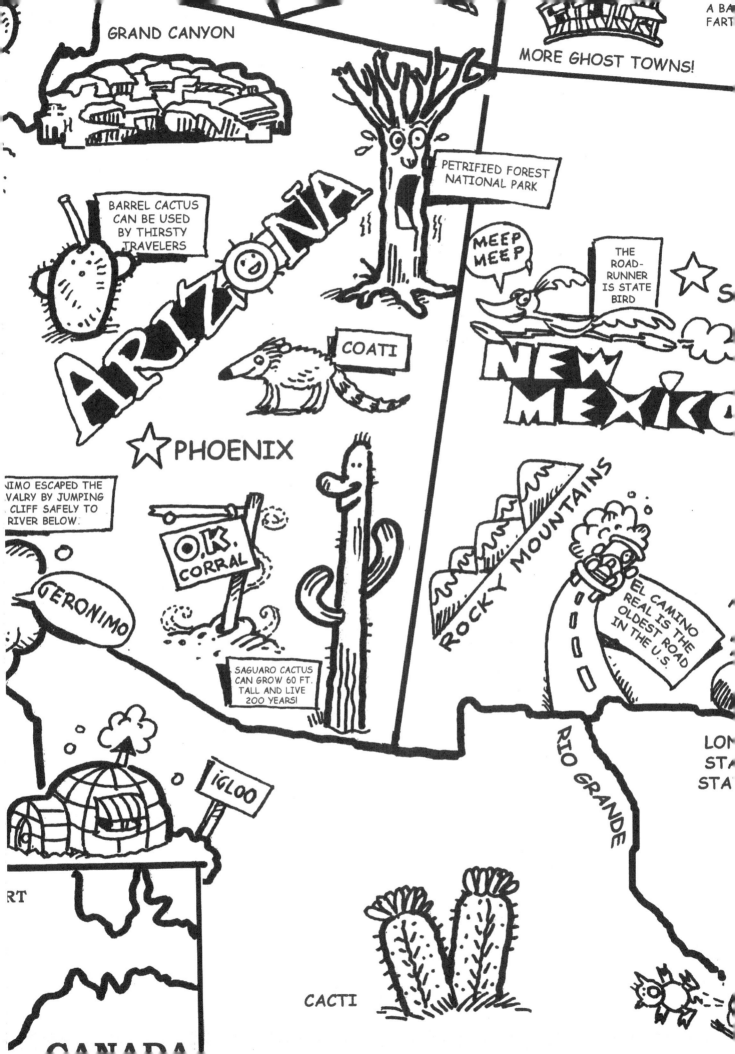

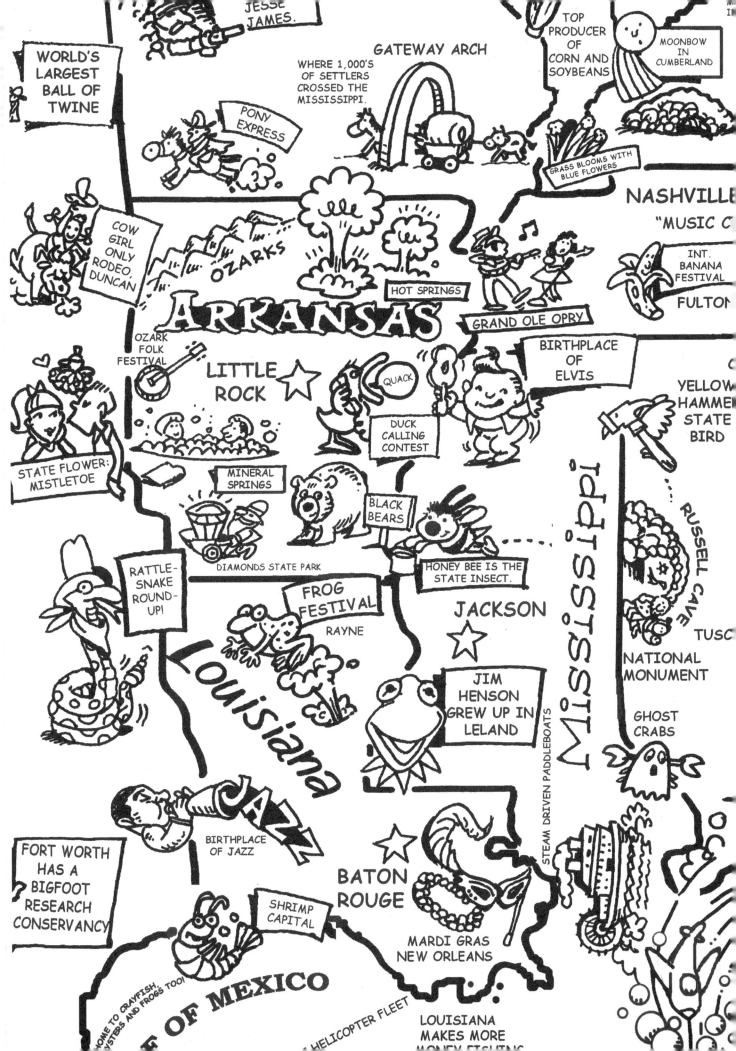

CRAB. DEL.

BLUE CRAB MD.

GRANDFATHER MOUNTAIN LINVILLE N.C.

1ST LOG CABIN CAME FROM SWEDEN

WRIGHT BROTHERS NATIONAL MEMORIAL IS IN KITTY HAWK, N.C.

DEL.

N. CAROLINA'S MANY PINE TREES MAKE A LOT OF TAR... WHICH CAUSES "TAR HEELS".

208 FT.

CAPE HATTERAS LIGHTHOUSE IS THE TALLEST IN THE U.S.

N. CAROLINA

POOF

ROANOKE ISLAND WAS THE 1ST ENGLISH COLONY IN 1587...A FEW YEARS LATER ALL COLONISTS DISAPPEARED... WITHOUT A TRACE!

TLE BEACH

N.CAROLINA 43 KINDS OF SNAKES!

ATLANTIC OCEAN

ALSO HOME OF THE KENNEDY SPACE CENTER

ANAVERAL

MT. McKINLEY
TALLEST U.S.
PEAK!

BERING SEA

SALMON

ANCHORAGE

PACIFIC OCEAN

PUFFIN

GULF OF
ALASKA

WHALE
WATCHING

ALASKA'S REAL NAME
IS ALAXSXAQ

PACIFIC
OCEAN

MONK SEAL

SEA TURTLES

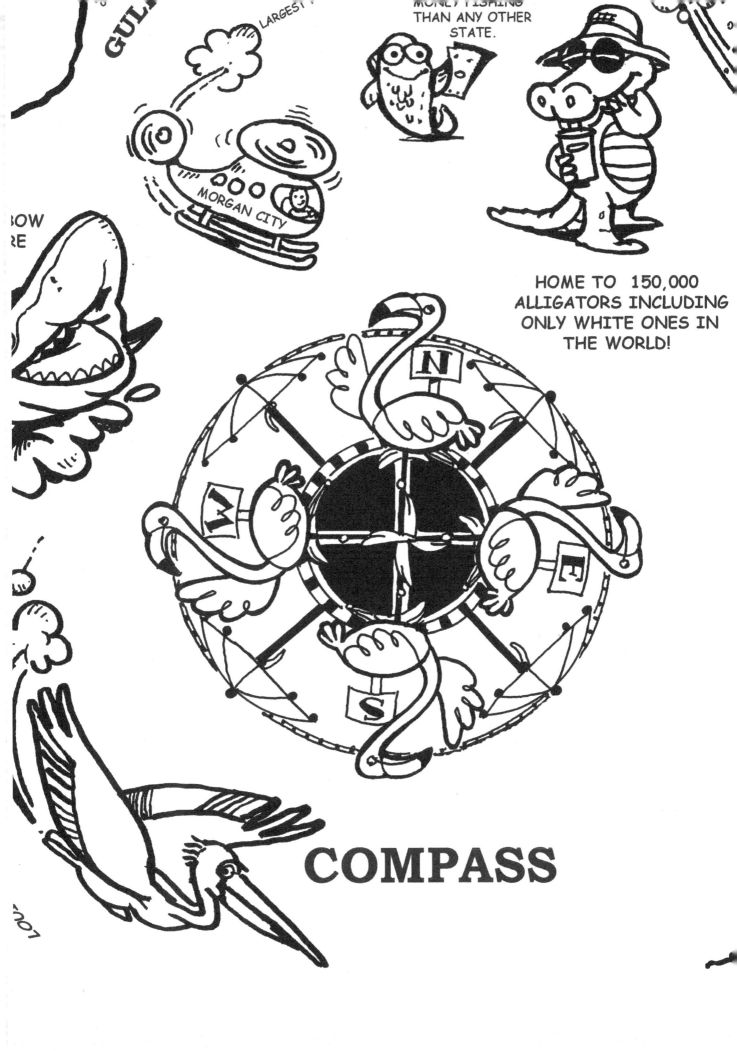

COMPASS

MEXICO

BLUE ANGELS
FLIGHT SQUADRON

SWORD FISHING

BREATHE
AND
CRAWL ON
LAND

RINGLING MUSEUM
OF CIRCUS HISTORY
SARASOTA

FLORIDA

THE EVERGLADES
HAVE ALLIGATORS,
BALD EAGLES,
AND COUGARS

FLORIDA KEYS

SEASHELLS

THIS IS A DRAWING
OF THE ARTIST OF
THIS BOOK.

SPONGE DIVING

CAN YOU FIND
THIS DRAWING
IN THE STATE
WHERE SHE
LIVES?

SURFS UP!

LORIDA GROWS
5% OF ALL
ORANGES
RODUCED IN
HE U.S.A.

THE ATLANTIC HURRICANE
SEASON LASTS FROM
JUNE 1ST THRU NOV. 30TH.

ONLY 1000 MANATEES
ARE STILL LIVING IN
FLORIDA WATERS

AMINGOS
N THE
RGLADES

DOLPHINS
ARE THE
SALT
WATER
MAMMALS
OF FLORIDA